COLLISION FORCES
Kath McKay

COLLISION FORCES
Kath McKay

All rights reserved. No part of this book may be reproduced, stored in a retrieval system or transmitted in any form or by any means electronic, mechanical, photocopying, recording or otherwise, without the prior permission of the publisher.

ISBN 9781903110287
First published in this edition 2015 by Wrecking Ball Press.
Copyright Kath McKay
Cover image: Edgley Cesar (http://creativecommons.org/licenses/by/3.0/)
Typeset by leeds-ebooks.co.uk
All rights reserved.

CONTENTS

Spot the Ball · 9
Palm Houses · 10
Nitrogen, carbon dioxide, oxygen, methane, hydrogen sulphide · 11
Must · 12
Fizz · 13
Cod Endings · 14
P. Lewis, trichologist · 15
Mustela nivalis · 16
Hook · 17
Volume 52, Issue 8 · 18
Landscape · 19
Stella Maris · 20
The Buddhist medal we found in my mother's drawer after she died · 21
Something Blue · 22
Ashes · 23
Light Waves · 24
Stroking an elephant · 25
Untitled · 26
Menú del día · 27
After Madrid · 28
If I had known · 29
Tomato sauce · 30
Tempest · 31
Light portion · 32
Your bare silver birch · 33
Your brothers give you back to me in Sydney · 34
I am swimming · 35
After the Stinger · 36
Niobe · 37
Just another man in a red jacket · 38

Traders · 39
Elonex word processor circa 1998 · 40
Double Land · 41
Goat in Snow (Le Brocquy, 1950) · 43
Seven · 44
One Body · 45
On the train to Hull reading Philip Larkin · 46
'Not much evidence of the docks' · 47
Fusion · 49
Again · 50
Hymn · 51
Hair, teeth, swimming · 52
Hieroglyphics on the Toll Bar · 53
In other news April 21st 2010 · 54
Room to let · 56
If you go · 57
God and aubergines in Roundhay Road · 58
In times of trouble and despondency... · 59
Cellophane Products · 60
October · 61
Ice · 62
Rowing across shallows · 63
The queue for fish · 64
La luciérnaga / The glow-worm · 65
The things they carried · 66
Working metal · 68
Translation 1 · 69
Translation 2 · 70
On the radio · 71
Acknowledgements · 73

COLLISION FORCES

SPOT THE BALL

Every Saturday for fifty years, my Saggitarius mother,
with a sharp tongue and a good line in put downs,
did Spot the Ball, ever since the only photo of her first-born
never developed. The photographer returned: 'Sorry, girl,
I'll take another.'

My sister was already in her coffin. Better to remember
her baby smell, the soft flesh of her buttocks, toothy grin,
the clearness of her skin. Better to sharpen skills on
Spot the Ball, focus on the distance of the arc from its
chord, work out where the arrow would fall.

PALM HOUSES

My parents visit Kew. They pay their penny, sit at the crossing
of Africa and the Americas. Banana trees, the fruit my father unloads.
'Musa acuminata' he mouths. 'Canary bananas.' 'Musa xparadisiaca,
enand gigante. Plantain.'

She, due to bear eight children, fingers dioscarea :
'a major contribution to the development of contraception'.
But this plant will be for her daughters and grandaughters.
She licks the sounds of custard apples: 'ananna cherimola.'

Children are calling in The Palm House. Cotton will unfold :
'Gossyium herbaceum, variety africanum'.

Back in Sefton Park, my parents linger near the Monsterosa Baja.
Panes of glass reflect them young and hopeful. They hold hands
on a bench, in sweaty humid air. Recite the names of ships:

Lusitania, Mauritania, Princess Royal. Their hands are dry,
hers from bannisters in big houses, his from flour sacks , asbestos.

He'll tell her of bananas as big as your arm, spiders, parakeets,
'and you should see the size of the rats.' Offers a cigarette. Gets
out a ring. She contemplates years of such polishing. Inhales.

NITROGEN, CARBON DIOXIDE, OXYGEN, METHANE, HYDROGEN SULPHIDE

Let's not forget Gaz, who always farted, air rising as we edged away.
When Mr Speyman asked for the square root of minus 5, and a definition
of Infinity, Gaz raised his hand. '25. Endlessness. As far up as anyone

can imagine, and then further.' Showed me once, his telescope
in the attic: *Andromedae, Leonis, Aquarii* .Pinpricks of light.
'SS Cygni. Crab nebula. Exploding balls of gas.' The rest of us

earthbound in terraces and semi-detacheds. Around him, air stretched
and bubbled with sulphur. *Atomic number 16. Atomic weight 32.07.*
Specific gravity, (rhombic), 2.07

MUST

I remember the must of my first library book: *Deciduous
Trees*. Spine broken, green with gold spots; book lice
crawling across my father's *The Cruel Sea*; the give
of a cracked leather sofa heavy with tobacco; the sight
of Arthur O'Connell shuffling out for the paper
in slippers and dressing gown; the taste of Fray Bentos,
the whoosh as steam escaped. The feel of her hand in mine,
dry boned, calloused.

FIZZ

After you dropped that last tab of acid, I bought chips. The Golden Fryer: grille on its windows, and *No More than three schoolchildren at one time.*

Examined each angle. The air fizzed. We each took a bite and something exploded. You rocked in the chair. All afternoon we sat as clouds filled the sky, and rain started up. Chips lost their heat. White blobs of lard congealed, hardening, like us.

COD ENDINGS

The factory hooter meant lunchtime up at Kraft,
where women streamed through gates, rushed home
to plonk beans or hooped spaghetti on the table.
At Birds Eye my mother stayed serving:
false teeth and smiles in the canteen.

Each night she'd bring home mis-shaped fish fingers,
those with extra batter, or thirteen in a box.
At lunchtime I had to open a tin.
Yet something of her was still in that kitchen
as battered cod sweated water on a plate.

Months later the factory hooter was a mourning call,
those mis-shapes a memory. All our fish fingers straight,
in proper boxes now, not curved like maps of Iceland,
cod endings becoming endings, the end.

P. LEWIS, TRICHOLOGIST

Down in entomology, there's a magnified louse on screen,
and the presenter's effusive about its claws:
'Perfectly adapted to wrap themselves round a hair!'

Behind are drawers full of bed bugs, fleas, wasps, tics
and aphids. A handwritten label: 'Head louse(Female)
Pediculus capitis P. Lewis, 102 Seel Street, Liverpool.'

A day in spring, just after the war. A client in for treatment,
and Lewis extracted a nit. Continued with the coconut oil
massage, advised lindane lotion.

After all day on his feet, he tweezed the ovum into a jar:
macerate, wash, stain, dehydrate, mount with Canada Balsam,
send the slide to the Microscopical Society . He liked looking

closely at things. Others were naming stars: far away
pinpricks, dots as small as the sugar he combed out
each day from sweating heads.

MUSTELA NIVALIS

I am wearing a rodent of beige fur.
With padded shoulders, already I feel taller.
Even when we found the jacket, as we rummaged
in Paddy's market, even when it smelt, Susan
could always see 'potential'. *Put it on,* she ordered.
Turn around. Twirl. Amongst the rags and bent over women
with bags and trollies, I did as I was told,
holding my breath against animal glue sweat.

Himalayan weasel. Mustela nivalis. She viewed me.
Suits you. Straightens you out. I sniffed.
Dry cleaning, she countered. *Worth it. It'll go
with your maxi.How much?* She haggled
with the Irishwoman who knew to a penny
what a person could pay. Later, on the bus,
the jacket in newspaper, people moved away from us .

After the cleaning, it was paler. I stepped
into it, as if it was a template. I had to stand taller.
All winter I lived in it, with long skirts and short,
trousers and dresses. Each night I hung it in the room
I shared with my sisters, and looked out at flatlands. I dreamt
of heights, where the earth met the sky.

It developed its own patina – beer, smoke, other things.
I left home in that jacket, holding the rail on the Belfast boat:
'I'll take you home again Kathleen.'
Already I stared past them. Eighteen.

HOOK

Each day I surfaced to the tread of your boots,
rose in the dark to make toast. You filled your gas bag:
white sliced, ham, a flask. And your hook.
Patinated wood, metal straight
and then curved like a question mark.

Silent, those mornings, the thin line of your lip
as you left for the bus stop. After, I'd curl
into bed for a half hour of reading,

while you, with that rictus grin, speared grain sacks,
hooked gas-fat bananas. I hooked my tongue
round other tongues.

One morning your hook still hung in the hall.
I took you tea. You didn't want a doctor:
'Only a cold.' For two weeks you coughed.

After they'd taken you, face under a blanket,
I pressed your hook into my palm,
watched blood start to pool.

Wednesday evening in Armstrong's printers, the junction
of English Scotch and Irish Street, Paddy laid out pages.
He held lino blocks, a scalpel. Wore a long leather apron.
Dark hair, blue eyes, pale, the one Catholic worker.
Every fortnight he set for us, in between gardening and army mags.
Behind us, rollers pressed out The Northern Ireland Builder.
Twelve pages done, Paddy moved onto Sports. *That there headline
needs a wee cut,* he said of the hockey story. *How's about
'Defeat Blow', sure?* At three a.m. we grinned.
Possibly we wouldn't make it. But Paddy sliced a leg
off the hockey team , fixed the photo in position, like a surgeon.
Right, that there's it. Photographed pages onto plates,
clipped them onto rollers, ready for the next shift.
Get yourselves away home, it's put to bed, so it is.
Heading out of English Street, we bombed down the motorway.
Past the lights of Long Kesh, into the Belfast dark.
Next morning, we'd be back, to pick up the five thousand.

LANDSCAPE

I show bare legs, in shorts that reveal the crack in my bum.
My belly is flat and pierced, light tanned, my hair long and curly.
When I widen mascara eyes, lads fall. I rub together lipsticked lips.
Move Maths class, above the boys. In Physics we discuss black holes

and negative numbers; collision forces. When the astronauts land on the moon,
Mr Digby has me explain: G forces; the Extra-Terrestial Exposure law;
the Apollo Lunar Receiving Laboratory; glovebox vacuum chambers;
the twenty-one days quarantine; how muscles turn to jelly.

After one night with a farmer's son in Wales, my first solo outing after passing the test,
there's a visit to a clinic in a Regency terrace. *It is the size of a fingernail,* I say.
I tell the boy nothing. In Edinburgh, reinvent myself. One boyfriend confuses
astronomy with astrology. Mockery is not a good trait, but helps me rise.

That summer the landscape opens up: the Söderfjärden plain in Finland:
'The result of a meteorite impact 520 million years ago,' says the Swedish guide:
'Sig landskapet.' Something stirs.

STELLA MARIS

Mary's statue reaches arms across the harbour
where boys dive into clear water
flecked with diesel .The ferry cuts through
The Narrows, lets its front down as it nears shore.
Cars start up. Two men in caps at the Cuan Arms
discuss Sean, who hasn't been over
for twenty years, but is just after getting back.

Hot whiskey slides down easy in November
when the sea mist rolls in and the long call
of the lifeboat breaks into your sleep. Inspectors
from England say the boat paint is toxic
to fish. Fungicides root, bed deep. This north
we're not without consequence . On clear nights
the Milky Way is visible, and a galaxy of stars;
Calisto and Cassiopeia, The Dog Star, The Plough

and at St Brigit's Well, rags on a hawthorn bush, alders,
scribbled wishes . Please God cure her,
Jesus grant my plea. In the cairns, boulders
cover stalagmites. Nitrates leach into the water
table. Fossils on the beach. On the shore
uprooted stones, people mumbling a prayer
say he went quick at the end, how people ought to.

THE BUDDHIST MEDAL WE FOUND IN MY MOTHER'S DRAWER AFTER SHE DIED

I wonder if it was the stillness that attracted her, after eight children.
All those mornings getting up: those breakfasts she prepared; those
pencil cases she filled; those lunch-boxes; the heads she had to brush;
the head-lice pick out or poison, those socks she had to wash, those
uniforms to iron, that sick she had to clean up, those spots to daub.
Calamine lotion. Aspirin . Junior Disprin. Gripe Water. Germolene.
'Eat your greens. Keep out of the sun with that skin.' Those scuffed knees
and scratched ankles, scabbed elbows. The endless wheel. So when
we finally slept, did she take out this medal? Extinguish her cigarette,
cross her legs, place her hands on her fleshless knees, straighten?
Om Mani Padne Hum. I think it was the stillness, and the promise
of water, maybe a few lotus flowers. *Black Narcissus, and the mad nun
with the lipstick.* Om. I hold the cheap silver, light as a grain of rice.
Only the hum of the fridge, the buzz of the switched off TV. Om.

SOMETHING BLUE

He has a face on him because we're sorting out photos
and there are none of him with my mother.
But you never took any.

We've been sitting up all night with my mother.
She's in her bedroom on blue satin, which matches
the Kensitas packet we've left in her coffin.

My sister in law leaves the bedroom. 'I had a cigarette
to keep her company.' My brother glares.
He blames my mother for getting him started, aged eight.

His job to light the first cigarette of the day from the stove.
Smoking became as natural as breathing:
It's taken him years. And on this day we burn her,

he's in a dark suit and white shirt, with empty hands.
Several of her twenty three clocks
have stopped, including the cuckoo one from Germany.

One sister takes this as a sign. Medicines, teeth and wig
are bagged up in the bathroom. A knock on the front door:
a Sikh guy offering to sell my mother another cardigan.

'You bastard,' shouts my brother. 'She's got a wardrobe
full of cardigans.' A police helicopter whirrs overhead.
A tap drips.

ASHES

After we threw my mother's ashes into the Mersey
we went to the Pier Head toilets to wash our hands.
An attendant in a 1940s pinafore, with long bangs
and dark lipstick like Baby Jane, said 'Sorry love,
the water's off.' Abseilers scaled the Royal Liver buildings.
We sucked ice creams. Rubbed hands with baby-wipes.
Licked our fingers.

LIGHT WAVES

Her twenty - six Amstrad Pal 1 Nicam Digital
Stereo/Teletext TV finally packs up.
The only way to get the picture right

was jump up and down in front of the screen
until Phil took a soldering iron to the cables,
while I got the brush ready, for electrocution.

Fuzzy lines, slo-mo ghost images, faded sounds.
Little of her left. The tape from her answer phone:
'I'll get back to you later'; a photo of her and an elephant;

a violin shaped clock; a couple in clover turning:
When Irish eyes are smiling; 'Do not overwind!!!'
We wait until Christmas Day. Four years.

'Fire and Shock Hazard. Do not expose to moisture.'
Drag to the wet garden. 'To prevent electrical shock,
do not remove screws.' Remove screws. Wires and circuits;

'Dangerous High Voltage. No user serviceable parts.'
Hold tendrils. 'Refer servicing to qualified service personnel.'
Raise hammers. *In sure and certain hope*

we commend you, 105/00 2285. *Commit you
to the ground*. Spread a cloth to catch shiny bits.
Light perpetual. Let go.

STROKING AN ELEPHANT

Green of course, the colleen's long dress, her with a wide straw hat, the man in knee-breeches, and a troubadour's hat. A shillelagh in his hand: 'When Irish eyes are smiling, there's a welcome there...' Round and round until they stop.

Five of her twenty seven clocks that never told the time; the switch that turns on the barking dog; the paper knife from Dublin; the sugar bowl from Blackpool, and the photo of her stroking an elephant, next to a keeper holding a pole.

Both smoking, yards from the elephant's sad gaze. My mother laughing like a Buddha. I like this tat, perched on a shelf in my newly painted house; this having a good time in the messiness of life; how everything can't be put straight.

I'd give you marshmallow bones in a hot dark tent,
dented foam mats ; that lightning chill on entering
the sea; at the Oasis, sieved rain on our heads,
surrounded by flats where people made tea; the smell
of burnt caramel in Lincoln's Inn Fields as coffee glasses
clinked and workers netted balls in company vests;
an afternoon film at the BFT, sweet as black market chocolate;
muscles shifting gear that June day on the Cam.
                                                          But I'd spare you from the asp dart
of headlice; the volcano of burnt skin; the jangle of toothache;
the scald of fingernails ripped off as the kitchen tap drips.

MENÚ DEL DÍA

Booked a hotel with a 'hairdresser' in every room, said *Hola*
to Esteban five times a day on the stairs, but sometimes it was
Tomás, who said *Buenas* and told us that Chueca, where Pilar lived
was full of hippies and that we should take care. *Precauciones.*
Scrambled eggs with prawns, hake and salad, ice cream.

Spent longer than I wanted in the bathroom. Fell down a hole
in the street, full of murky black water, trooped up past Esteban,
smelling of drains. *Pásate, pásate,* he smiled. Scrubbed off black gunk
with yellow soap that smelled of childhood.
Perfect fried aubergines. Grilled salmon, fried potatoes. Flan.

Wrapped a blanket around myself at three in the morning while others
got ready to go out, cars tooted below and in a doorway two fighting drunks
kissed. Grave waiters span bread, wine and water onto tablecloths.
Heard the pad of monjas descalzadas : barefoot nuns.
Broad beans. Hake medallion, fried potatoes. No pudding.

Came in on the maids talking about us hanging clothes on the balcony.
Heard the shouts of Guernica, saw arms flung back, a head, mouth open,
a donkey braying, a piece of the cross. Felt the moth breath of a pickpocket
on Sol. *Your bag is open señora.* Moved everything to the front.
Mixed salad. Cod. Chips. Yogurt in its supermarket carton.

In the Prado saw Italians cluster round St Bernard receiving miraculous
lactation from the Virgin, mouth opened to a long stream of bright light.
Banners on balconies were 'contra la guerra'. Another Madrid 'es posible'.
'Against the noise. Eight months without sleep'. 'Our children are ill. Justicia'.
Gazpacho. Tuna in tomato sauce. Cheese and crackers at Pilars.

Patatas bravas, pimientos de padrón, gambas al ajillo, tortilla, pizza marinera.

AFTER MADRID

I forgot to tell you that I picked up a shell that day on Filey Beach,
with the hang- glider overhead, and now when I hold the periwinkle
to my ear I'm at the pork farm we stopped at just off the A64, the one
with the happy pigs. You ate a whole pork pie: that night had chest pains.
The start of a summer of scans, breath tests, taking blood. We'd only just
started leaving our daughter on her own, on those seaside days out
she no longer wanted to go on. Later that summer, after sharing yet another
room, she told us she was never going on holiday with both of us ever again.

IF I HAD KNOWN

that October Sunday at one o'clock was the last ,
I would have picked somewhere better
than aisle fourteen of Tescos to not say goodbye.

Tesco Crisps 79p. Frozen Prawns. Pappadum Plain
Semi Skimmed M Small Notebook Small Notebook Small Notebook.

Instead, with our daughter tugging at me for Top Shop
I piled the groceries on you, sped off to buy her a jacket
too loose, which two weeks later I returned.

I'll remember our goodbye as earlier that day
when leaving me half naked in bed,
something made you turn at the door,

come back and kiss me on the lips, tuck bedclothes in.
As if you knew that from that night on ,
I'd be in our bed alone.
As if to say *Ride On My Love Ride On.*

TOMATO SAUCE

The day after, I scoured the freezer for evidence, scorched my mouth
on chilli. Later, in the darkened room you'd suckled me in,
I snuffled into your Hawaiian shirt, soaking it in snot I refused to wash off.
A helper brought tea I cradled like kryptonite.

The following days we tried. Our son used mushrooms and carrots.
I fried onions in sunflower, not olive. None chopped garlic and onions
so fine, none stewed them transparent, none cut up tomatoes
so small, extracted the stalks, none simmered it for hours, like you

that winter evening, waiting for me to come home to your pasta
with tomato sauce, your offering.

TEMPEST

I wish I didn't have to meet him,
but I give him tea in our living room
and biscuits, even though we hardly ever have biscuits.

Right now we've got a houseful of biscuits,
people keep giving us biscuits, making biscuits.
I can't taste anything except curries.

He has a list of questions. He's discreet about the tickboxes.
And he's good, very good. Body language appropriate.
Puts his hands together as if praying,

looks me in the eye, but doesn't hold my gaze too long.
That would be creepy. He leans forward in empathy
and nods as I speak. We are getting through something,

making a plan. And the day is sliding away,
like I thought days never would again.
But I'm most impressed with the grey curls

sprinkling from his head like from a watering can.
A middle aged Botticelli angel. Curls clean and bouncy.
If you touched them, they'd spring back.

'I'm here for you,' he says. 'I'm here.'

LIGHT PORTION

Lying on the black IKEA sofa you died on, I'm reading about Newton's first law of motion. Midnight, Friday. I've watched Black Books. A customer tried to buy 'real leather-bound' Dickens from Bernard, 'to go with his sofa.'

By now I would have curled into you and a book. Einstein says the time lapse between two events depends on the measurer's perspective. Sometimes you're dead yesterday. Sometimes you're still here. But always it's the hour of walking

down the street to our house, a police car outside. Always it's the hour of you still on our sofa. Old Spanish for body is 'la ponderosa porción', the soul 'la leve porción': 'light portion'. I press the rewind button. Hold my stomach.

YOUR BARE SILVER BIRCH

In the park, your bare silver birch. My locked spine, mouth at an angle,
pain in my gum. The bed without you. My face white without makeup.
The playground empty.

Six in our unit, one down. Me parading as a child, a sixer
in the Brownies. Six Day War, and you in England then.
The Six Counties, where I lived.

A girl on a pink bike laughs, and the park ripples.
I worry at the inside of my tooth with my tongue,
willing my gum to pink up , like our son who didn't cry
after birth: Apgar score 3/10. That nothing else will be lost.

Your tree is not dead, only storing up energy for the winter.
Like me, with my hat on. Underneath, still things going on.
Robins covering a grave. The mouse the cat tossed in the air.
Twigs, lightbulbs.

YOUR BROTHERS GIVE YOU BACK TO ME IN SYDNEY

in an orange flowered box: your letters from England,
Annapurna, Istanbul, Kabul.

1974 and you're holed up in Camden. 'I can't imagine
another winter here.' Next autumn we bed down in Hackney.
You write to Oz 'The difficult part of the day is over,'
as children sleep . Details of their asthma, quirks and school.

Friends take your ashes on a speedboat at Pittwater.
Ten in a five person boat, so five lie down, pursued
by Water Police. Michael, barefoot, with long
grey hair, speaks of the end of your physical body.

Kate claims a beam of light 'at the exact spot' the ashes tip in.
On shore, Tony complains. 'Too many bloody ashes,
Pittwater's filling up with bloody ashes.'
I sift through the box.
Your first Communion, baptism , music report aged eight.

'Surprising how much progress Phillip has made
On so little work.' Pictures of you rowing, in shorts,
posing in puppy fat adolescence before you lengthen and thin.

Put into orbit.

I AM SWIMMING

I am swimming in the waters of your childhood.
Every morning at Manly, after the white robed elders
leave the harbour pool. People jog, walk dogs;
you're here in that fixed look in Pab's eye,
Michael's slight stammer. In how they say 'swimmers'
for trunks; 'costumes' in the plural,
their insistence on 'juices' as the best part of a meal,
how talk turns to compost. Blue vests on the ferry,
that Aussie 'OK'. I'm swimming on the harbour-side,
you'd be in surf. Every morning I wake before our daughter,
swim in the waters of your childhood. Re-learn.

AFTER THE STINGER

After the stinger, Maureen says 'Get back
in the water and swim. Like riding a bike.'
This after phoning the emergency department in Perth,
them saying 'Vinegar. How do you feel in yourself?'
This after heat and swelling on my back,
a red, pulsing wound.
Next morning I step into clear water.
Fish tickle my feet.

NIOBE

At times I'd rather be a Niobe, a stone running water,
but as Emma says, 'Food has to be put on the table,
socks still need sorting.' So black and white, and shades
of grey, we go through them one morning in a sisterly way.
I press my lips against your photo frame.
Unknot my shoulders. Eat.

JUST ANOTHER MAN IN A RED JACKET

When I looked back along the seafront, you
were jollying us along , happy our boats weren't plastic,
laughing that any fool could see candles would not light
on a North Sea beach in April. Daffodils, though tacky,
'at least are grown in North England.' Pleased
that we dug our hands in and sprinkled you
into paper boats, passed them out to Catherine
standing like Jesus in her rolled up jeans in the sea.
And some bobbed back and some sailed off.
On second glance you were just another man
in a red jacket. One of our crew.

TRADERS

At the University Antiques Roadshow, I'm told *They're not worth much. Probably belonged to a Chinese trader from Tibet, who saddled his horse, filling them with provisions or water.*

Brown leather, round, long tassels, images of the tao scoured in orange and white, now stabled in your study.

I put my nose in, sniff batteries, a bike pump. Imagine traders asking after families, before they got onto business: *How is your grandfather? And son. Your wife. How is the weather in your part of the world?* Rice, silk, spices exchanged.

I wake from a dream where my feet are cut off. You left the saddlebags to our son. Were you trying to say *Trav*el, *go forward. Take the roundabout route. Talk to people. Trade.*

ELONEX WORD PROCESSOR CIRCA 1998

Boxy as a Soviet car, it took up two thirds of my desk,
while others slimmed down, became pencil like.
This bod had to warm up. Every day rebooted seven
or eight times. Always in danger of losing

work. Fatal errors commonplace. When the nerd
said 'It's reached its time,' I shed no tears. He fiddled
with wires and circuits, pressed a few buttons, transferred
contents to my laptop. Numbers and symbols

passed. *Programme in operation.*
Years panned from one computer
to another. Ninety-seven; ninety-eight; ninety-
nine; two thousand; two thousand

and one; two thousand and two. A blip.
Two thousand and three whizzed on.
Later I scoured the hard drive for your bank statements, spread sheets,
calendars: something of you coiled deep.

The new flat screen squats on my desk. The monster
is on a half way shelf, with the Lexmark printer
that proved incompatible, the faulty Epson Stylus
Color 760 , the broken 5000,

the Webrider, the electric typewriter, the Fontwriter,
the Dell keyboard, the old fax,
the Amstrad. Their memories.

DOUBLE LAND

The woman annoying in two languages sits at the back of the coach
on the way up to The Pinnacles, translating for her French party.
They don't need words to feed the kangaroos at the wildlife park,
one with a joey in its pouch, that pops its head out to eat pellets.
Or to stroke the spreadeagled wombat on its keeper's knee,
or to see the koalas who almost fall off their perches
as the guide explains about koala sex.

She's not a thin woman but she's telling our guide
about her new system for losing weight.
'I have never felt so well.' She keeps on talking,
all the long way past trees and the wheat belt, up, up
into the desert. We arrive at a collection of tin huts called Cervantes.
The French people have paid fifteen dollars extra to eat rock lobster.
There's a layer of sand over everything.
Tea is one dollar a plastic cup, the milk is uncovered.

Flies everywhere. Postcards and dried bottle brush for sale,
Australian calendars, tea tree oil, soap and emu oil.

Back on the coach one of the French people spews up,
and the woman annoying in two languages sprays disinfectant down the aisle,
like men in khaki shorts did the first time I landed in Australia.

People sleep, or look out at desert. No trees, no shadow, and when we get out
at The Pinnacles, even she quietens. How small we are. Rock formations
in the shape of a kangaroo, a man meditating, a wombat, a penis.
The guide walks us through the sand, says he's never lost anyone 'yet.'
A Japanese man tries to photograph the wind.

The woman annoying in two languages hushes. No more about her husband,
or business, how 'insanely' they are working. Back towards Perth,
desert gives way to banksias and wattle trees. My eyes play tricks.
I see darting aboriginal figures in this 'dune-like land with trees and bushes,'
the first Dutch settlers named; this slechtlandt / badland; this heuvelich landt /
hilly land; this 'low land like drownland '; this Dubbel Landt / Double Land

GOAT IN SNOW (LE BROCQUY, 1950)

Green eye flirts, eyelashes twitch.
Black slit like the line in the centre of a banana,
angled eye turns, flickers. Pyramid bags fold.

The wing of the machete, a grey flow
of cape, a wide rictus. Bridge strength.
The tip of the scales. A yoke. Bones.

The udder like a fifth cloven foot.
Ice cream cone, grey froth meeting pink
muscle below flesh, fat. A red shadow.

The airbrush of a tail like an egg beaten by a whisk,
the spring held up behind, a length of thick rope,
the scrag end of the body, the afterthought. A rustle of air.

SEVEN

That seven is the least number of times you have
to shuffle cards in order to shuffle them properly.
That this is a truly a Treasure Island, East of Eden,
made by a Blind Watchmaker, who looks down on
The Bone People, late night on Watling Street.

In The Nine Tailors locks rise over the Fens
and bodies are found bloated, face down.
Lock keepers can tell the age of a corpse
by the state of decay.

    It's a good holiday this,
though the inventory lists a kettle I've never
seen the like of. It works, but we can't get much
use for the waffle maker. In the paper was a man
holed up against the Water Authority. Refused
to pay his water rates, said water was free,
collected it in buckets.

    Because of the shotgun
they sent in the police. Twenty years. Leicester. He studies
ornithology, knows a great crested grebe from a sandpiper,
the migratory patterns of geese, even though he's thirty
miles from water and not going anywhere.

    Villains in the pub, on a break
from Islington. A canoe club on flat water. High squeaky girls
Please Sir Go On Sir Tell us Sir Can we do this stretch of water Sir.
And it's a real East of Eden, a Treasure Island, made by a Blind
Watchmaker, looking down on The Bone People, rabbiting
and carousing Late Night on Watling Street.

ONE BODY

Sylvia tells me that in Headingley Baptist Church
They go in for total immersion. None of this
wetting of the head and a few drips of water
but bending the body over, pushing the person
into the baptistery : one, two, three
and the church, full of twenty and thirty year olds with mobiles,
holds its breath. One, two, three and the person surfaces,
face streaming and the minister sets a light
behind the newly baptised. Their face glows.
Opens his hands: 'I am the resurrection and the light.'
Leads the stunned congregation out to see chionodoxa.
The glory-of-the-snow.

ON THE TRAIN TO HULL READING PHILIP LARKIN

and everything is luminous. The man in the spring raincoat
who always goes the toilet just after Selby, wears his face
as if something, like anything, might happen today.
The man in the brown trenchcoat stands at the door, fingers
on the button, looking at his watch. The Humber swirls off
to Barrow and New Holland. Spouses kiss their partners
goodbye, bikes spill into the corridor, as if coupling.
Two lads bang on about Final Frontier, Level 1, 2 and 3:
'If you tackle the first one.'

The woman who gets on at Howden sits with her legs apart,
reading a Metro: 'Staffie cross toddler savage.' And then
the harp strings of the bridge lift our hearts. Now we're by
the lucent comb of the Infirmary. Staff smoke behind bins.
We see into sample rooms. Today some will climb
the highest floors. Streetlamps go off, lights are dimmed
on bikes and cars. The sun comes up. The in-box, meetings,
lunch. An evening drink with friends. Domes and spires.

'NOT MUCH EVIDENCE OF THE DOCKS'

Take a figure of eight. Wind back round yourself.
Like a Moebius strip.

Pilot's Way. Isis Court. Ocean Boulevard.
Plimsol Way. Harbour Way. Helm Drive.
The Haven. The Citadel: the strongest fort in Britain,
never taken.

Below the Citadel, foundations.
The Winding Shed. Close your eyes.
Haul up the pulley. Tick tock. The engine thrums.
Ropes get purchase on a ship. Ease it into dock.

On the foreshore a man saws branches off an ash tree,
chops them into logs. With his son, wheelbarrows home.
A terrier yaps and snaps. Joggers in bright colours ballet through.

Mast Drive, Sailor's Wharf, Spinnaker Close. A bench
at Pettingell's View. You'd see the ferry to New Holland.
Corinthian Way. A lone lad in a hoody at the bus stop.
Marine Drive. Navigation Way. Galleon Court.

Houses with room for the kids. Who'd go back to the hot breath of cattle?
Toxic sludge from the Timber Ponds, sterilised and built on.

We loop back on ourselves: Tobacco Dock; Coal Dock; Flapgate; Half-tide Basin.
Fever Hospital; Coal Crane. Tick-tock. No trains stop at Victoria Dock.
Even the supermarket's Spar. Water percolates.

The pavement ends. Unfenced gravel and mud, unevenness. Wrecked jetties by Alexandra Dock, a warehouse falling into the sea. *Pride of Rotterdam* in the distance. Sandpipers picking at snails and worms. Danger signs. Blue lights, klaxons. A metal bridge rises, releases a barge to chug ash up the estuary. Slow time. That fat sun over the Humber. That wind looping back on itself.

FUSION

Late Sunday afternoon, I sellotape straws up the backs
of paper dolls from a Chinese shop in Madrid.

Mount figures on cardboard: still they fall over. Cut out
clothes: the girl in a fifties full skirt, the boy in ironed slacks.

Rods in their backs, like you. Your daughter fixes screws
in a mirror you'll surface in, stiff and unbending, yet taller.

Lying flat, you watch with your grandkids. Bones fuse.
Adolescent, you should have spent a summer like this,

prone in a close, shuttered room, cartilage taken from your hip,
corseted and kept level. Franco wouldn't bow out. You pushed off,

and curved. As your spine twisted and buckled, you headed north:
Copenhagen, Amsterdam, London.

Now with your body going south, you've let surgeons get their hands
on you. Set you straight.

AGAIN

This Sunday morning in the Place des Batignolles, cygnets with yellow and grey down block our path. A notice on a poplar tree warns 'Danger de Mort.' Coots flap in branches. Cyclists circle the park. A waterfall drops. At Bassin St Louis, tents line the towpath, a police van revs its engine. Here, joggers retrace steps, and a woman herds children into a pink plastic tent: the Petits-Guignols. 'This way for the show. Le voleur du petit-singe.' Boys fall backwards off their chairs. 'Restez bien, les enfants.'
The artist marionette steals the petit-singe from the zoo. The policeman whacks him with a truncheon. Asks the children what to do. 'Au Prison' they shout. 'Tout de suite'. The policeman drags him off: In the Bassin St Louis, van doors open.

HYMN

I'm on the roof terrace of the Pod Hotel on East 47th Street
and a small child is doing the Downward Dog near the safety rail.
Her father sips white wine. Columns loom up like Tetris,
the air languid. We eat aubergine salad, hummus, flat bread.
Nina cracks open Prosecco, and we toast: New York, this April night,
the kid doing yoga,
                    a father on the subway persuading his four-year old
to a playdate at a car showroom. 'It'll be real fun, won't it?'
'No,' she answers, and the whole carriage whoops.

Praise what exactly? That big wide basketball player offering a seat
with the politest 'Ma'am'; the woman who breathed 'Have a
wonderful day';the man on crutches who asked 'Would you
permit me?' and the girl before us in the TV show queue, who
cheered as the security guard let us both in, pushing us into
the last seats in a studio warm with lights.

                                'Go,' he shouted, as outside,
horses pulled carriages, dropping their shit into bags, filling the air
with richness, something worth praising.

HAIR, TEETH, SWIMMING

You talk about your children.
His are younger than yours.
Scan neutral topics - hair, teeth, swimming,
the break up of the coal industry.
He throws out 'maybe we could...'
Unused to reading signs, you block him.
Prattle on. He talks about his mother, how
she phones up to ask what he's eating.
He still has a mother. Plates widen.
Heat crawls over your skin.

HIEROGLYPHICS ON THE TOLL BAR

Every week on the allotment we'd forget what we'd done.
Every week like starting again. The capital of Paraguay.
Richard of York gained battle in vain. The ablative case
in Latin and Russian. Brassicas. Judías. Wrong language.
Taking the roundabout route to remembrance. Did we plant beans?

Asking Graham about the new plants poking through: *Some kind of cabbage*,
he'd always say. *Why don't you put sticks in, write their name on?*
Later found rain-sodden sticks, hieroglyphics. N X h 11 T l 2 ([])
Gardening as cacography. When others joined our group they'd sow seeds

and then get deported to Africa. Every Saturday an adventure of spindly corn,
Pak Choi, oriental radishes. Potatoes were easy, but those curly things
with serrated edges? Fed them to the family for weeks.

IN OTHER NEWS APRIL 21ST 2010

On the seventh day after the skies filled with ash, when we walked at Far Ings, a helicopter over the Humber Bridge brought the first workers back from North Sea oil rigs, and an Eastern Airways T3752 took off for Aberdeen.

... redwings were still present: fourteen feeding on the southern roadside pastures. A late flock of fieldfare... regular appearance of kingfisher after the 16th. '2 together on 20th'. Very encouraging

A clear day: sun, cool wind, a woman in a red vest running along the shore, terrier yapping at her heels, a man surfacing from a hide in Gore-Tex and mountie hat, with a tri-pod and binoculars.

'The bitterns are booming,' shouts the Visitor Centre worker. The shush and shish of waves over brown silt and clay, the Hull to Leeds train on the opposite bank, a laden cargo boat heading for the estuary.

The chirr-chirr trr of sedgewarblers, who never sing the same song twice, two mute swans at the outflow at Chowder Ness. Discarded cans of Fosters and Carlsberg Export in trodden down weeds, red pantiles transversely curved to ogee shapes, double continuous curves, never touching.

First Chiff Chaff on the 21st... within five days five birds singing... Sand Martin: Dusk watch on the 24th... gathering of seven escalate to a roosting flock of 50 within the last hour and a half of light

Cirrus clouds, silver bullet trucks charging over the bridge, a lone cyclist pedalling against the wind. 11,000 tonnes of steel mesh bending and shifting.'Things they found when they excavated the bridge: Clews, flatties, layers of shells, a human skeleton.'

Swallow... first one of spring on the 24th. By 31st twelve over Ness Pitt. House Martin: single bird.

'The planes are back,' says a man with a stick. Far above a small aircraft leaves the first contrail for a week. I read that flocks of birds sometimes attempt the Humber Bridge several times, puzzled.

Cetti's warbler, Woodcock, Barnacle short-eared owl, Barn owl, Avocet, Peregrine, Little Egret ,Grey Wagtail, Bearded Tit... intensifying relationship between a regular male and a female Marsh Harrier

ROOM TO LET

No, I am not going to input my details into the Wells Fargo bank.
We have no space for a piano or organ. It is not a lively household.
I will not calculate the direct debit, or make myself available

in a manner conducive to your daughter's education.
No more enquiries please. There is no bed, only a picture of a bed.
My daughter banged a peg in the wrong hole. We have no pliers.

I will probably have to buy a new bed. I've been immersed
in IKEA instructions for weeks, and looking at the cartoon
of a grumpy man holding a phone, without any enlightenment.

IF YOU GO

To the top of our
house there is
a pipe with a crack in it which
drips over the
back wall outside
the kitchen, making the
walls wet and rotten.
One day I'll climb up
and fix that bastard.
When the weather was cold
the honeysuckle became solid
beautiful and useless.
And now that the wall's newly painted
blisters of paint fall to the floor
our wages turning to dust.

GOD AND AUBERGINES IN ROUNDHAY ROAD

Already mad at God, I take him down the back alleys to Roundhay Road.
'I mean, look at this mess,' I say to him. Pizza boxes erupt out of bins.
'Disgusting.' But he points out a child on a bike, and I notice that Sandra
is planting out her summer bulbs. She waves, tells me she's been meditating:
her face glows. Down the alley near the Greek church there are needles,
turds. Oi Trei Hierarchi have a wedding on. Women with dark hair
in flouncy dresses, small boys in suits.

Down past Abu Bakars I take God, inhale the smell of naan bread.
To the Persian tea house for mint tea.
At Arti's restaurant a couple share dhosas, and then we're in
the post office queue: '£50 to the Central African Republic.'
'Four first class stamps.' 'A parcel to India.'

In the grocers, I buy bananas and a handful of chillis, garlic, ginger.
Squeeze an aubergine. Look at God. Mango juice, pistachios.
'See,' I'm saying, as we bite into samosas at Bobby's.
God seems to like the yoghurt sauce. Under a Coronation photo of the Queen,
one brother measures out pakhoras, nods over as if he knows us, smiles.

IN TIMES OF TROUBLE AND DESPONDENCY...

... I go the cinema in the afternoon. I've watched some awful films in my time. Sometimes there's only four people in the cinema, and we nod and eye each other warily.

'Do you know where the toilets are?' is acceptable, but anything further and you're hitting on them, or worse, want to discuss the film.

I get to see lots of obscure French, Spanish and Eastern European films, mostly about people hating each other, or misunderstanding each other, or about to get their big break. Something always goes wrong – they don't get out of bed in time, or they attempt one last robbery. People have dark rings round their eyes, and smoke a lot, shrug their shoulders. There is usually a bastard of a barman, or world-weary at least, who makes pronouncements about the meaning of life.

Afterwards when you come out, blinking into the afternoon light, you feel as if you have been to confession.

... I also go swimming. You need a costume, swimming hat, goggles, ear plugs, a quiet time of day for clear lanes: mid – morning or mid afternoon. Wednesday evenings in the summer are full of people trying to get fit for their holidays. Don't go during school lessons.

Keep your head under most of the time. Don't look anyone in the eye. Don't get behind a guy with a float, or one doing his back exercises who is actually going a different way to the rest of us, or one doing backstroke who can't read arrows.

Take the word 'Slow Lane' with a pinch of salt. There are few men in the slow lane. They are all in the fast lane, going slow.

Use a deceptively relaxed stroke. Stretch out. Notice the pattern of light through the sixties brutalist windows. Ignore the crud – plasters, broken wrist bands, brown bits. Ignore the cockroaches, the ceiling parts that drop into the water, the scrabbling on the roof. Ignore the rat that looks in once, heading off towards the yoga class.

Find a clear patch. Swim until your legs ache. Think of nothing. Keep breathing.

CELLOPHANE PRODUCTS

I queue outside Huddersfield Central Post Office.
As a Russian, I am used to closed doors. 'Open
9-5.30. Except Saturdays and emergencies.'
Friday 9.15: a list of emergencies pinned to the wall.
'The manager's cat died ,' someone whispers.
In Russia, this is covered in a thick book of regulations:
'Compassionate leave due to bereavement/closest associates.'
Section thirty-two, subsection 8a.

'The cat only ever came near him to bring another corpse.'
On the Siberian steppes, my relatives drink vodka
to stay warm. Several were found frozen where standing.
My uncle got his feet amputated. 'Yto Eto?' I ask a woman
who slugs back a bottle of vodka. 'You what?'
Looks like a relative: pot belly, papery red skin,
thin hair, missing teeth. I am the other side of a mirror.

In the market I queue for bruised apples, and 'Cellophane Products'.
'What is these cellophane products?' 'You taking the piss?' Nyet.
I catch Russian words: Starsky; Smirnoff; Bolshoi; Vodka; Sputnik.
Toothless women in the café claim sugar lumps are 'good for the brain,'
like babushkas pouring black tea from samovars on the Krasnodar train.
In the pound shop, I buy a chocolate head of Lenin. An East wind blows.
At the Russian baths, a fat woman with big breasts beats me.
I have to pay for this.

OCTOBER

Promise of cold. Each morning harder to move our limbs.
The alarm rings, we snuffle into bedclothes.
I head down past wet leaves on the pavement
two years ago I took a fall on. Got the handlebar
in my chest. In the park dealers are shuffling.
The street women look up, pull their coats.
Drivers toot horns. I remember that Zeus
tied Prometheus to a rock in the sea. Each day
an eagle tore out his liver. Each day it grew back.

ICE

That first time our son fell through the ice,
you wrapped him in your coat and Russian hat,
rode him past people looking daggers .

Tried to sneak him in. His face was blue.
I turned round and he was under the ice.
Surprised as you were when bees stung my lips.

We didn't know then how easy it is for children to fall
from one element into another. At 4.30 his coughing wakes me,
the morning as cold as the day he first fell through the ice.

ROWING ACROSS SHALLOWS

You're just in the swim of things, paddling up and down
minding your own business, unaffected except
for the occasional influx of water through goggles,
when the news strikes you. At 41, Anne's dead.
You swim anyway and notice that you are moving
from the slow lane to the medium
and even there overtaking people. The long glide before dying.
Underwater you hold your breath, wonder about the sensation
of drowning, remember how in The Perfect Storm, it says everything
clouds over and pain gives way to an unreal dark sensation
as the brain shuts down, how a child can be revived
after thirty or forty minutes, two hours. You've been reading
about Russia and frozen lakes, spent yesterday morning
unfreezing your daughter's water bottle you'd spent all night freezing.
By the time you've finished swimming, Anne's still,
somewhere in St Albans and back in the library,
the slides of the Catholic saints she catalogued,
lie silent. St Aidan rows across shallows to Holy Island.
Books continue to get stamped, magazines put away.
Someone starts to unravel Anne's computer files. The library
rings with silence and a stench of rubber, as a fluorescent light
burns out. Outside, daffodils mock us. Time.

THE QUEUE FOR FISH

Look the speaker in the eye
but don't hold their gaze too long
or they'll think you're weird.
Appear 'nice'.

Be aware of the effect you're having on the speaker.
Ask them lots of questions. Laugh
at appropriate points, give them encouraging nods
to faff on about themselves.

Afterwards they'll claim you're interesting,
although they haven't asked you a single question
about yourself and fail to recognise you in the queue for fish.

They keep the fishmonger a long time, playing to the audience.
Someone from the back of the queue starts shouting,
'Why don't you get a fuckin boat, if you're so fuckin interested in fish?'

and you know that this particular slice of real life will feature
in their next performance, to show they're still in touch
with the grass roots, and you want to say Skate. Tuna. Headless reds.
Snapper. Octopus. Salmon. But you ask for three pieces of coley
and think that sometimes being invisible has its advantages.

LA LUCIÉRNAGA / THE GLOW-WORM

While Thomas struggles to breathe in San Cecilio Clínico,
Liz carries a glow- worm down from La Alpujarra. Cradles it
like the newborn she once gave to the light.

Back at the house, the green light fades. We read that the last three
abdominal segments of lampyridae consist of a layer of protein,
called luciferin, backed by a reflective layer of minute crystals.
Light is produced by enzymatic oxidation.

After near drowning, Thomas is breathed for in Granada.
He was born underwater, the caul still around him.
A glow-worm turns off its light by decreasing the air supply.
We will the glow on. Switch on your lamp, we pray.

THE THINGS THEY CARRIED

Katie carried black socks she'd just bought in Streatham High Street for 2.99.
John carried a pot of miniature daffodils. The invite said no flowers.
Eileen carried photographs of Callum she pinned on the walls.
Glyn carried Rebecca on his shoulders. She kept asking 'Where's Callum?'
Joan, the grandmother, carried shortbread biscuits and Tesco tea bags
and some of the holy oil the priest had given her when Frank died.
The grave-digger carried a shovel.
Jane carried a copy of the collected Eavan Boland.
Terry carried tapes of Christy Moore and Paul Robeson.
Clare carried a bible she hadn't looked at since her teens.
Rosie carried a skipping rope. She was going to do
a skipping rhyme for Callum , but when she saw all the people
in the hall, she grew shy and nuzzled into Eileen.
Father Tom carried a copy of the service and the weight
of the congregation . Siobhan from Canada carried whiskey
for afterwards, Anne from South Africa carried letters from women
in her family expressing sorrow 'for your deep sad loss'.
Laurie carried crocus bulbs, Marcus carried balloons.
Tim carried a copy of Tolstoy's short stories.
Nurse Sewell who worked in Guys carried a copy
of Callum's certificate 'for being brave during his operation'.
Rebecca carried her dummy. She lost it several times.
Michael, his uncle, carried a list of children who'd slept
in Callum's cot –Rosie, Rebecca, Maria, Ellie, Eavan .
Some people carried babies. Some carried bags
from Leeds, London and all over the Midlands.
Some carried nappies, baby food, government papers, train and plane
timetables, tickets, address books, letters, memorial cards.
Helen and Kevin carried Callum's small white coffin.

Sean carried earth from Ireland which he passed round
to sprinkle on the coffin. They all carried their voices, quietly at first,
but then loud as the yellow of the balloons,
the children released from Callum's grave.

WORKING METAL

I could lay out her knives, forks and spoons
From one end of her house to the other.

Unused fishknives encased in blue velvet,
teaspoons with ivy curled up their spine,
'Thomas Hinchcliffe -"*Master Cutler*"' sugar spoons,
solid plain meat knives. Pudding spoons, soup spoons.

Elastic from knickers twisted together with other elastic
to make string. Unravelled carpets wound round cards,
under eaves in the attic.

Macramé instructions. 1940s utility dress patterns.
Buttons: football, shell, four hole, two hole, shiny, matt.
Every letter I wrote her. A list of letters
Of the alphabet I knew aged five.

Her grandmother clock, silver hairbrushes.
Her grandmother's brooches.

After the funeral, I work metal up the Humber
with Sam , an ex-miner, who coaxes filigree ostrich eggs
from metal strips so fine you can hardly see the joins.

In my dead mother's house, my brother's shirt crumples.
He buys an ironing board cover.
Opens a kitchen drawer. Six ironing board covers.
New, still sealed.

TRANSLATION 1

When the wind blows in off the North Sea, caravan walls shake
and swimmers in the pool shiver.
A lone man in a wet suit surfs out towards the bar.
I follow his figure with a thermos.
There are ice-breakers heading for Russia,
hailstones as big as cats.
If he gets past Spurn Head, he will fall off the edge of the world,
and into the next one, warmed by Caribbean currents,
where dead children from the East gain colour,
and people speak in tongues with upward inflections,
not these hard separate words, packed dense as snow.
As ends.

TRANSLATION 2

I have walked down these roads all my life.
The pale shadows of my ancestors burn me.
When I enter the new clearing ,
the moon drops out of the sky .

For my children, hopes are baskets.
They play on sands in this new moon.
Turn and dance young birches of spring.
Circle round the ice that melts.

ON THE RADIO

There's something on the radio about head turning:
a scientist who's spent two and half years
in international airports, watching people turning their heads
towards loved ones. Whether they go right or left.
Excludes those carrying parcels.
I turn my head.

ACKNOWLEDGEMENTS

Thanks to editors of the following publications, where some of the poems, sometimes in different versions, were first published: *Telling the Bees* (Smiths Knoll), *The Rialto*, *Interland* (Smith Doorstop), *Not in So Many Words* (Smith Doorstop), *Humber Writers' anthologies* (Kingston Press), *Magma, Brand, Mslexia, Red Ink, Swarm* (Wellhouse Publications).